GOD Is Infinite Blessings!

God's Eternal Gifts to You

Glen R. Landin
Gail A. Reffert

Copyright © 2015 Glen R. Landin.

No part of this publication may be reproduced or transmitted in any form or by any means, electronic or mechanical, including photocopying, recording, or by any information storage or retrieval system without written permission from the publisher.

CREATIVEARTISTIC PUBLISHING
ORANGE, CALIFORNIA

ISBN-10 0996280707
ISBN-13 978-0-9962807-0-9

PRINTED EDITION: APRIL 2015

PRINTED IN THE UNITED STATES OF AMERICA

WWW.GLENLANDIN.COM
WWW.CREATIVEARTISTICPUBLISHING.COM

This Divine book entitled, "GOD Is Infinite Blessings! – God's Eternal Gifts to You," is comprised of inspired scripture of who God is. There are 301 attributes and each one has several scriptures to accompany them. There are also Bible and dove silhouettes on alternating pages. The note pages leave room for you to find more attributes about God. This book can be used for churches, pastors, and for your own personal growth in creating a beautiful relationship with our Lord Jesus Christ.

Dedication

This book is dedicated to our one, true Lord Jesus Christ and The Holy Trinity which consists of The Father, The Son, and The Holy Spirit. This book is for God-fearing people and God-seeking people everywhere. These divine words will touch hearts and souls around the world.

GOD IS INFINITE BLESSINGS!

God is A Joyful Noise
Psalms 98:4, Psalms 100:1

God is Abba
Mark 14:36, Rom. 8:15

God is Able
Matt. 12:29, 1 Cor. 4:10

God is Abundant
Proverbs 12:11, Matt 6:33

GLEN R. LANDIN – GAIL A. REFFERT

God is According
Genesis 17:3, Psalm 95:6

God is Alive
Romans 7:9, Mark 16:11

God is All Powerful
Genesis 18:18, Joshua 4:24

God is Alleluia
Psalms 107:50, Revelation 19:1

GOD IS INFINITE BLESSINGS!

God is Almighty
Genesis 17:1, Job 27:2

God is Alpha
Isaiah 41:4, Revelation 1:8

God is Always on Time
Ecclesiastes 3:3, 2 Corinthians6:2

God is Always Right
Job 40:2, 2 Timothy 4:2

GLEN R. LANDIN – GAIL A. REFFERT

God is Always There
Deuteronomy 31:8, Hebrews 13:5

God is Always with us
Deuteronomy 1:27, 1 Kings 8:57

God is Amazing
Proverbs 30:18, Joshua 3:5

God is Among Us
Mark 10:43, Matthew 20:26

GOD IS INFINITE BLESSINGS!

God is Answerable
Psalms 145:18, Hosea 2:6

God is Armor
Hosea 2:16, Ephesians 6:11

God is Astonishing
Genesis 1:1, Psalms 46:8

God is Atmosphere
Genesis 1:1, Revelation 21:1

GLEN R. LANDIN – GAIL A. REFFERT

God is Available
1 Samuel 21:4, Luke 2:7

God is Awe Inspiring
John 1:1 Revelation 22:1

God is Awesome
Job 37:22, Isaiah 64:3

God is Awestruck Wonder
Jonah 1:16, Matthew 9:8

GOD IS INFINITE BLESSINGS!

God is Beautiful
Isaiah 52:7, Romans 10:15

God is Beginning
Genesis 1:1, John 1:1

God is Beholder
Genesis 25:11, Job 7:8

God is Beside Us
Malachi 2:10, John 1:14

GLEN R. LANDIN – GAIL A. REFFERT

God is Blessed Assurance
Isaiah 32:17, Hebrews 6:11

God is Blessing You
Deuteronomy 7:13, James 1:12

God is Blessings
Luke 17:13, Luke 24:30

God is Blood
1 Corinthians 10:18-22, 1 Peter 1:18

GOD IS INFINITE BLESSINGS!

God is Body
Genesis 12:7, Matthew 1:23

God is Boundless
Genesis 1:1 Philippians 4:16

God is Bountiful
Psalms 65:11, Proverbs 22:9

God is Bread of Life
Luke 22:15-20, 1 Corinthians 10:19

God is Breath
Job 33:4, 2 Timothy 3:16

God is Breathtaking
Genesis 1:1, Hebrews 1:3

God is Brilliant
Exodus 34:5-7, Ephesians 4:24

God is Builder
Genesis 1:1, Hebrews 3:4

GOD IS INFINITE BLESSINGS!

God is Caring
1 Timothy 5:4, James 1:27

God is Carpenter
Matthew 13:55, Mark 6:3

God is Carrying Us
Exodus 14:11, Exodus 33:15

God is Choices
Romans 6:23, Matthew 7:13-14

GLEN R. LANDIN – GAIL A. REFFERT

God is Circle of Life
John 15:13, John 10:10

God is Comforter
Isaiah 40:1, 2 Corinthians 4:1

God is Commitment
Matthew 16:24, Luke 9:23

God is Communion
Acts 2:42, 1 Corinthians 10:16

GOD IS INFINITE BLESSINGS!

God is Compassionate
Psalms 103:8, Joel 2:13

God is Complete
John 15:11, Colossians 4:17

God is Conscience
1 Corinthians 10:29, 1 Timothy 11:5

God is Continually
Deuteronomy 11:12, 2 Chronicles 9:7

GLEN R. LANDIN – GAIL A. REFFERT

God is Cornerstone
Ephesians 2:20, 1 Peter 2:6

God is Cosmos
John 3:16, Romans 8:10

God is Counselor
Isaiah 40:13, Romans 11:34

God is Creation
Romans 1:20, Colossians 1:15

GOD IS INFINITE BLESSINGS!

God is Creator
Ecclesiastes 12:1, Isaiah 43:15

God is Dazzling
Song of Solomon 5:10, 1 John 1:5

God is Deep
Psalm 42:7, Luke 5:4

God is Deity
Jeremiah 23:23, Colossians 2:9

GLEN R. LANDIN – GAIL A. REFFERT

God is Deliverer
Psalm 70:5, Psalm 144:2

God is Dependable
Psalm 19:7, Isaiah 33:16

God is Determined
Lamentations 2:8, Zechariah 8:14

God is Divine
Isaiah 35:4, 2 Peter 1:3

GOD IS INFINITE BLESSINGS!

God is Emmanuel
Isaiah 8:8, Matthew 1:23

God is Endless
Genesis 1:1, Revelation 1:8

God is Enough
Exodus 9:28, Proverbs 3:10

God is Eternal
Titus 1:2, 1 Peter 5:10

GLEN R. LANDIN – GAIL A. REFFERT

God is Everlasting Life
Daniel 12:2, John 5:24

God is Everything
1 Corinthians 15:27, Hebrews 2:8

God is Every-when
Esther 9:28, Romans 14:11

God is Everywhere
Mark 16:20, Luke 9:6

GOD IS INFINITE BLESSINGS!

God is Exalted
Psalm 46:10, Matthew 23:12

God is Excellent
Psalm 45:2, 1 Corinthians 12:31

God is Exceptional
Psalm 115:15, Daniel 6:3

God is Extraordinary
Daniel 5:12, Act 19:11

God is Faith
Hebrews 11:1, Acts 17:11

God is Faithful
1 Thessalonians 5:24, 1 John 1:9

God is Fantastic
Job 36:3 Psalm 95:6

God is Father
Luke 15:20, John 15:1

GOD IS INFINITE BLESSINGS!

God is Favor
Proverbs 12:2, Isaiah 61:2

God is Flesh
John 1:1, Ephesians 6:12

God is Forever Lasting
1 Corinthians 13:8, 1 John 2:17

God is Forgiving
Matthew 6:14, Luke 6:37

God is Foundation
Ezra 3:11, Revelation 21:14

God is Free
John 8:36, Romans 6:20

God is Friendship
Proverbs 22:24, James 4:4

God is Fullness
Romans 11:12, Ephesians 4:13

GOD IS INFINITE BLESSINGS!

God is Fun
Luke 6:25, Acts 2:13

God is Future
Jeremiah 29:11, Matthew 6:33

God is Generous
Matthew 20:15, 2 Corinthians 9:5

God is Gentle
Matthew 21:5, 1 Chronicles 4:21

GLEN R. LANDIN – GAIL A. REFFERT

God is Gift
Romans 5:16, Acts 11:17

God is Giver of Life
Genesis 2:7, Deuteronomy 20:16

God is Glorious
Deuteronomy 28:58, Palm 72:19

God is Glory
Exodus 15:11, Ecclesiastes 33:22

GOD IS INFINITE BLESSINGS!

God is Good
Genesis 2:9, Joshua 23:14

God is Grace
Psalm 45:2, Proverbs 22:11

God is Gracious
Psalm 148:8, Isaiah 30:18

God is Great
Genesis 39:9, Deuteronomy 7:21

GLEN R. LANDIN – GAIL A. REFFERT

God is Great Emanator
Deuteronomy 11:8, Judges 16:5

God is Greater
Genesis 29:9, 1 John 5:9

God is Guaranteed
Genesis 44:32, Romans 4:16

God is Hallelujah
Revelation 19:1, Revelation 19:6

GOD IS INFINITE BLESSINGS!

God is Happiness
Ecclesiastes 2:26, Matthew 25:21

God is He Is
Acts 4:12, 1 Timothy 2:5

God is Healer
Exodus 15:26, 1 Corinthians 12:28

God is Health
Proverbs 3:8, Mark 2:17

GLEN R. LANDIN – GAIL A. REFFERT

God is Heaven
Genesis 2:4, Deuteronomy 31:28

God is Heavenly Host
Psalms 103:21, Luke 2:13

God is Helpful
Acts 20:20, 2 Timothy 4:11

God is High Priest
Leviticus 16:32, Leviticus 21:10

GOD IS INFINITE BLESSINGS!

God is Highest
Matthew 21:9, Luke 19:38

God is Holy
Genesis 2:3, 1 Chronicles 16:35

God is Holy Spirit
Matthew 28:19, Acts 2:4

God is Honor
Psalms 84:1, 1 Timothy 1:17

God is Hope
Job 8:13, 1 Peter 1:21

God is Hosanna
Matthew 21:9, John 12:13

God is I AM
Exodus 3:14, Psalm 46:10

God is Immanite
Isaiah 55:8, John 1:1

GOD IS INFINITE BLESSINGS!

God is Immanuel
Isaiah 8:8, Matthew 1:23

God is Immeasurable
Genesis 1:1, Ephesians 3:20

God is Important
Mark 12:29, Luke 20:46

God is In Control
Job 37:15, Jeremiah 28:14

GLEN R. LANDIN – GAIL A. REFFERT

God is Incarnate
John 1:14-18, 1 John 5:1

God is Incredible
John 14:6, Acts 26:8

God is Infinite
Genesis 1:1, Ephesians 3:18-19

God is Inspiring
Psalms 3:2, Proverbs 3:5

GOD IS INFINITE BLESSINGS!

God is Invisible
Romans 1:20, 1 Timothy 1:17

God is Jealous
Exodus 20:5, Joshua 24:19

God is Jehovah-Gmolah
Number 34:1, Jeremiah 51:6

God is Jehovah-Jireh
Genesis 22:14, Matthew 6:25

God is Jehovah-Nissi
Exodus 17:15, Psalms 20:5

God is Jehovah-Rafha
Exodus 15:25-27, 2 Kings 20:1

God is Jehovah-Rohi
Psalms 23:1-3, John 10:14-18

God is Jehovah-Shalom
Isaiah 9:6, Proverbs 18:21

GOD IS INFINITE BLESSINGS!

God is Jehovah-Shammah
Genesis 36:13, 2 Samuel 23:11

God is Jehovah-Tsidkenu
Jeremiah 23:6 Jeremiah 33:16

God is Jehovah-Yahweh
Exodus 6:3, Isaiah 12:2

God is Joy
Deuteronomy 16:15, Ecclesiastes 11:9

GLEN R. LANDIN – GAIL A. REFFERT

God is Judge
Genesis 31:53, Hebrews 4:12

God is Justice
Deuteronomy 16:20, Isaiah 30:18

God is King
Genesis 35:11, Revelation 16:14

God is Knowing
Genesis 3:5, Genesis 3:22

GOD IS INFINITE BLESSINGS!

God is Leader
Exodus 34:31, 2 Timothy 3:16

God is Leading
2 Samuel 15:2, Matthew 26:55

God is Life
Genesis 2:7, 1 John 1:4

God is Light
Genesis 1:3, Exodus 10:23

GLEN R. LANDIN - GAIL A. REFFERT

God is Light of the World
Matthew 5:15, John 8:12

God is Limitless
Job 42:2, Philippians 4:13

God is Listener
Proverbs 21:28, James 1:19

God is Living Color
1 Chronicles 29:2, Revelation 21:21

GOD IS INFINITE BLESSINGS!

God is Living Water
Jeremiah 2:13, John 7:38

God is Lord of Hosts
2 Kings 21:5, 2 Chronicles 33:5

God is Love
Exodus 15:13, 1 Corinthians 13:1

God is Loyal
2 Samuel 3:8, Colossians 3:23

GLEN R. LANDIN – GAIL A. REFFERT

God is Magnificent
1 Kings 8-13, 2 Chronicles 6-2

God is Majesty
Exodus15:7, Deuteronomy 5:24

God is Maker
Genesis 1:1, John 1:1

God is Mankind
Genesis 6:7, Deuteronomy 32:8

GOD IS INFINITE BLESSINGS!

God is Marvelous
Psalm 71:17, 1 Chronicles 16:24

God is Master
Genesis 24:27, Genesis 24-56

God is Me
Judges 3:10, Luke 24:45

God is Measureless
Revelation 1:8, Revelation 22:13

GLEN R. LANDIN – GAIL A. REFFERT

God is Mediator
Romans 8:26, 1 Timothy 2:5

God is Mediation
Psalms 19:14, Psalms 104:34

God is Merciful
Deuteronomy 4:31, Psalms 4:1

God is Messenger
Job 1:18, Proverbs 16:14

GOD IS INFINITE BLESSINGS!

God is Messiah
John 1:41, John 4:25

God is Mighty to Save
Isaiah 63:1, Zephaniah 3:17

God is Mind
Deuteronomy 28:65, 1 Chronicles 28:12

God is Ministry
Acts 1:17, 2 Corinthians 3:9

GLEN R. LANDIN – GAIL A. REFFERT

God is More
Deuteronomy 28:11, Job 36:28

God is Most High
Psalm 7:10, Daniel 4:2

God is Moving
Genesis 1:21, Matthew 21:21

God is Everything
Genesis 1:30, Psalm 28:7

GOD IS INFINITE BLESSINGS!

God is My God
Genesis 28:21, Exodus 15:2

God is My Hero
Exodus 3:8, Psalm 22:21

God is My Testimony
Job 19:25, 1 John 5:11

God is Mysterious
Daniel 2:30, Ephesians 3:3

GLEN R. LANDIN – GAIL A. REFFERT

God is Near
Genesis 49:22, Leviticus 21:17

God is Necessary
Acts 1:21, Hebrews 9:23

God is Never Ending
Genesis 21:33, Psalm 111:10

God is Noble
Exodus 24:11, Isaiah 13:2

GOD IS INFINITE BLESSINGS!

God is Obedience
Exodus 19:5, 2 Corinthians 10:5

God is Ocean
Genesis 1:2, Revelation 13

God is Omega
Revelation 1:8, Revelation 22:13

God is Omega Omani
Jeremiah 13:23, Nahum 3:9

GLEN R. LANDIN – GAIL A. REFFERT

God is Omnipotent
Genesis 1:1, Hebrews 1:3

God is Omnipresence
Genesis 3:8, Psalm s 139:7

God is Omnipresent
Psalm 139:7-12, Matthew 6:1-18

God is Omniscience
Psalm 139:1-6, Isaiah 40:13-14

GOD IS INFINITE BLESSINGS!

God is Omniscient
Psalm 139:1-6, Isaiah 40:13-14

God is One
Deuteronomy 6:4, Ephesians 4:6

God is Opulent
Genesis 1:1, Psalm 50:10

God is Original
Ezra 2:68, Hebrews 3:14

GLEN R. LANDIN – GAIL A. REFFERT

God is Outstanding
Psalm 62:11, John 4:24

God is Oxygen
Ezekiel 37:9, Ecclesiastes 3:19

God is Parental
Ezekiel 18:20, Proverbs 17:21

God is Passion
Acts 1:3, 1 Corinthians 7:9

GOD IS INFINITE BLESSINGS!

God is Patience
Isaiah 7:13, 2 Timothy 3:10

God is Peace
Isaiah 26:3, Philippians 4:7

God is Perfect Timing
Ecclesiastes 9:12, 2 Corinthians 6 : 2

God is Perfection
2 Samuel 22:31, Job 37:16

GLEN R. LANDIN – GAIL A. REFFERT

God is Perpetual
Exodus 29:9, Leviticus 3:17

God is Planets
Psalm 8:3, Psalm 19:1

God is Planner
Job 15:32, Isaiah 30:8

God is Plentiful
Matthew 9:37, Luke 10:2

GOD IS INFINITE BLESSINGS!

God is Potter
Isaiah 29:16, Jeremiah 18:4

God is Powerful
Genesis 1:1, Luke 24:19

God is Praise
Genesis 29:35, Judges 5:3

God is Prayer
Job 22:27, 1 Thessalonians 5:17

GLEN R. LANDIN – GAIL A. REFFERT

God is Precious
Proverbs 3:15, Isaiah 43:4

God is Precise
Jeremiah 33:3, John 16:24

God is Preparing
Genesis 1:1, John 1:1

God is Present
Psalm 46:1, Isaiah 43:12-14

GOD IS INFINITE BLESSINGS!

God is Prince of Peace
Isaiah 9:6, 2 Thessalonians 3:16

God is Promise
Deuteronomy 31:6, Hebrews 13:8

God is Prophet
Amos 3:7, Romans 1:2

God is Protector
Psalm 46:11, Isaiah 25:4

GLEN R. LANDIN – GAIL A. REFFERT

God is Proven
Romans 5:4, 1 Peter 1:7

God is Provider
Genesis 49:20, Psalm 54:4

God is Pure
Proverbs 10:20, Philippians 4:8

God is Radiance
Habakkuk 3:4, Hebrews 1:3

GOD IS INFINITE BLESSINGS!

God is Reassuring
Psalm 112:6-8, Hebrews 13:5

God is Redeemer
Isaiah 47:4, 1 Chronicles 17:21

God is Refuge
Psalm 18:2, Psalm 46:1

God is Relationship
Psalm 19:14, Revelation 21:3

GLEN R. LANDIN – GAIL A. REFFERT

God is Rescuer
Jeremiah 30:17, Luke 24:4-8

God is Resplendent
Isaiah 14:12 Revelation 22:16

God is Restoration
Jeremiah 30:17, Joel 2:25-26

God is Resurrection
Luke 24:4-8, 1 Thessalonians 4:14

GOD IS INFINITE BLESSINGS!

God is Revealer
Psalm 19:1, Daniel 2:47

God is Righteousness
Matthew 6:33, Romans 4:3

God is Ruler
Psalm 103:19, Nehemiah 9:6

God is Sacrifice
Isaiah 57:7, Romans 12:1-2

GLEN R. LANDIN – GAIL A. REFFERT

God is Salvation
Matthew 8:18-22, Romans 8:38-39

God is Sanctify
Genesis 1:27, Jeremiah 1:5

God is Saving
2 Samuel 22:36, Psalm 22:1

God is Savior
1 Timothy 1:1, Titus 3:6

GOD IS INFINITE BLESSINGS!

God is Second Adam
John 3:16, 1 Corinthians 15:45-47

God is Self-Appointed
Matthew 21:23, John 5:36

God is Sent
Mark 6:7-12, Luke 10:1

God is Shepherd
Psalm 23:1-6, John 10:14

GLEN R. LANDIN – GAIL A. REFFERT

God is Significant
John 3:16, 1 Peter 2:9

God is Silent
Psalm 46:10, Luke 1:20

God is Solar System
Genesis 1:1, Revelation 21:1

God is Son
Isaiah 9:6, Luke 2:11

GOD IS INFINITE BLESSINGS!

God is Sovereign
Genesis 15:2, Judges 6:22

God is Speaking
Genesis 11:6, Exodus 19:9

God is Spirit
John 14:26, Romans 8:26

God is Still
Psalm 37:7, Psalm 46:10

GLEN R. LANDIN – GAIL A. REFFERT

God is Strength
Psalm 46:1, Isaiah 49:29

God is Supplier
Judges 19:20, Philippians 4:19

God is Supreme
Zephaniah 3:17, Ephesians 2:4-5

God is Sustainer
Genesis 27:37, Psalm 55:22

GOD IS INFINITE BLESSINGS!

God is Tabernacle
Exodus 26:26, Exodus 36:14

God is Teacher
1 Timothy 4:13, 2 Timothy 3:16

God is Terrific
Genesis 1:16, Genesis 18:18

God is The Gate
John 10:7, John 10:9

GLEN R. LANDIN – GAIL A. REFFERT

God is The Great I AM
Exodus 3:14, John 8:56

God is The Highest
Numbers 14:40, Job 22:12

God is The Lamb of God
John 1:29, Revelation 5:6

God is The Lord of Hosts
Psalm 24:1-2, Psalm 148:2

GOD IS INFINITE BLESSINGS!

God is The One
John 10:30, John 14:6

God is The Originator
Genesis 1:1, Jeremiah 1:5

God is The Path
Job 22:15, Psalm 77:19

God is The Rock
Genesis 49:24, Exodus 17:6

GLEN R. LANDIN – GAIL A. REFFERT

God is the Same Forever
Psalm 136:1, Hebrews 13:8

God is the Same Today
Luke 23:43, Hebrews 13:8

God is the Same Tomorrow
Exodus 9:5, Hebrews 13:8

God is the Same Yesterday
Job 8:9, Hebrews 13:8

GOD IS INFINITE BLESSINGS!

God is The Way
Genesis 3:24, John 14:6

God is There
Deuteronomy 31:8, Joshua 1:5

God is Timeless
Genesis 34:19, 2 Peter 3:8

God is To Come
Daniel 7:13, Matthew 24:30

GLEN R. LANDIN – GAIL A. REFFERT

God is Trinity
Genesis 1:26, John 1:1

God is Trustworthy
Exodus 18:21, Psalm 119:86

God is Truth
Psalm 145:18, John 14:6

God is Unchanging
Hebrews 6:17, Hebrews 12:17

GOD IS INFINITE BLESSINGS!

God is Understanding
Deuteronomy 1:13, Judges 13:18

God is Unity
Psalm 133:1, John 17:23

God is Universe
Ephesians 4:10, Philippians 4:15

God is Unlimited
John 6:51, 1 Timothy 1:16

GLEN R. LANDIN – GAIL A. REFFERT

God is Unpredictable
Isaiah 6:10, Luke 19:40

God is Victorious
1 Chronicles 15:54-57, Revelation 2:7

God is Watching Us
2 Chronicles 16:9, Jeremiah 1:12

God is Weather
Genesis 8:1, 1 Kings 18:45

GOD IS INFINITE BLESSINGS!

God is Whenever
Ruth 1:16, Mark 14:9

God is Wherever
Ruth 1:16, Mark 14:9

God is Whole
Genesis 1:29, 1 Thessalonians 5:23

God is Wisdom
Proverbs 4:7, 1 Corinthians 1:21

GLEN R. LANDIN – GAIL A. REFFERT

God is Wise
1 Corinthians 3:18, Matthew 10:16

God is With Us
Joshua 1:9, Matthew 1:23

God is Wonderful Counselor
Psalm 138:6, Isaiah 9:6

God is Word
Psalm 119:11, John 1:1

GOD IS INFINITE BLESSINGS!

God is Working
1 Corinthians 12:5, Colossians 2:23-24

God is World
Exodus 34:5-7, Deuteronomy 20:4

God is Worthy
1 John 1:8-9, Revelation 4:11

God is Zealous
Deuteronomy 4:24, 1 Corinthians 6:20

GLEN R. LANDIN – GAIL A. REFFERT

The Books of the Old Testament

Genesis	Proverbs
Exodus	Ecclesiastes
Leviticus	Song of Solomon
Numbers	Isaiah
Numbers	Jeremiah
Deuteronomy	Lamentations
Joshua	Ezekiel
Judges	Daniel
Ruth	Hosea
1 Samuel	Joel
2 Samuel	Amos
1 Kings	Obadiah
2 Kings	Jonah
1 Chronicles	Micah
2 Chronicles	Nahum
Ezra	Habakkuk
Nehemiah	Zephaniah
Esther	Haggai
Job	Zechariah
Psalm	Malachi

GOD IS INFINITE BLESSINGS!

The Books of the New Testament

Matthew	1 Timothy
Mark	2 Timothy
Luke	Titus
John	Philemon
Acts	Hebrews
Romans	James
1 Corinthians	1 Peter
2 Corinthians	2 Peter
Galatians	1 John
Ephesians	2 John
Philippians	3 John
Colossians	Jude
1 Thessalonians	Revelation
2 Thessalonians	

GOD IS INFINITE BLESSINGS!

The 10 Commandments

1. Thou shalt have no other gods before me.
2. Thou shalt not make unto thee any graven image.
3. Thou shalt not take the name of the Lord thy God in vain.
4. Remember the Sabbath day, to keep it holy.
5. Honor thy father and thy mother.
6. Thou shalt not kill.
7. Thou shalt not commit adultery,
8. Thou shalt not steal.
9. Thou shat not bear false witness against thy neighbor.
10. Thou shalt not covet.

GLEN R. LANDIN – GAIL A. REFFERT

Psalm 23

The Lord is my shepherd, I lack nothing.
He makes me lie down in green pastures,
He leads me beside quiet waters,
He refreshes my soul.
He guides me along the right paths
for his name's sake.
Even though I walk
through the darkest valley,
I will fear no evil,
for you are with me;
your rod and your staff,
they comfort me.
You prepare a table before me
in the presence of my enemies.
You anoint my head with oil;
my cup overflows.
Surly your goodness and love will follow me
all the days of my life,
and I will dwell in the house of the Lord
forever.

GOD Is Infinite Blessings!

The Lord's Prayer

Matthew 6:9-13 (KJV)

Our Father Which art in Heaven
Hollowed be THY Name,
They Kingdom Come.
THY will be done in Earth as it is in Heaven.

Give us this Day our Daily Bread.
And Forgive us our Debts,
As we Forgive our Debtors.

And Lead us not into Temptation,
But Deliver us from Evil:
For Thine is the Kingdom
And the Power and the Glory For Ever.
AMEN.

GLEN R. LANDIN – GAIL A. REFFERT

GOD Is Infinite Blessings!

GLEN R. LANDIN – GAIL A. REFFERT

GOD Is Infinite Blessings!

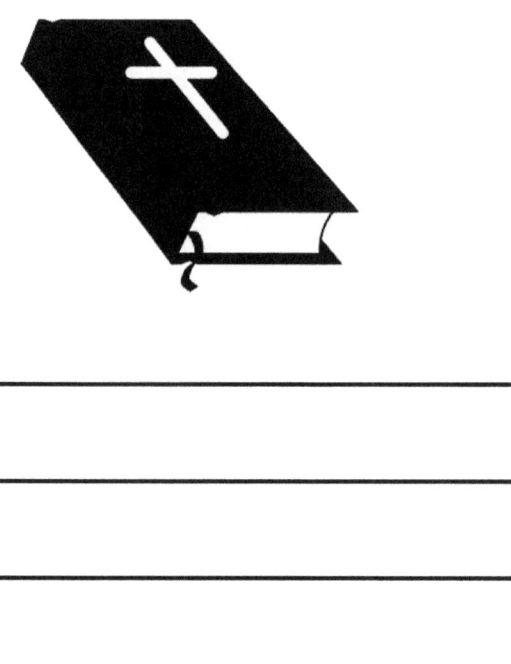

GOD Is Infinite Blessings!

_____

_____

_____

_____

_____

_____

_____

GLEN R. LANDIN – GAIL A. REFFERT

GOD Is Infinite Blessings!

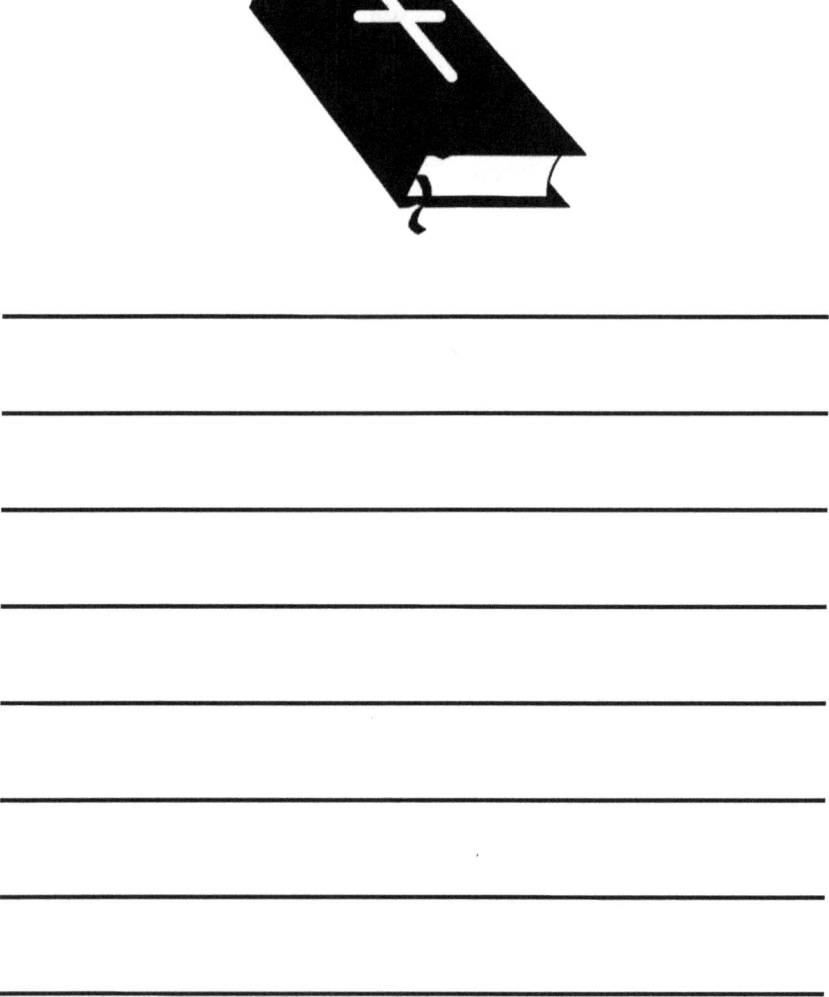

GLEN R. LANDIN – GAIL A. REFFERT

GOD Is Infinite Blessings!

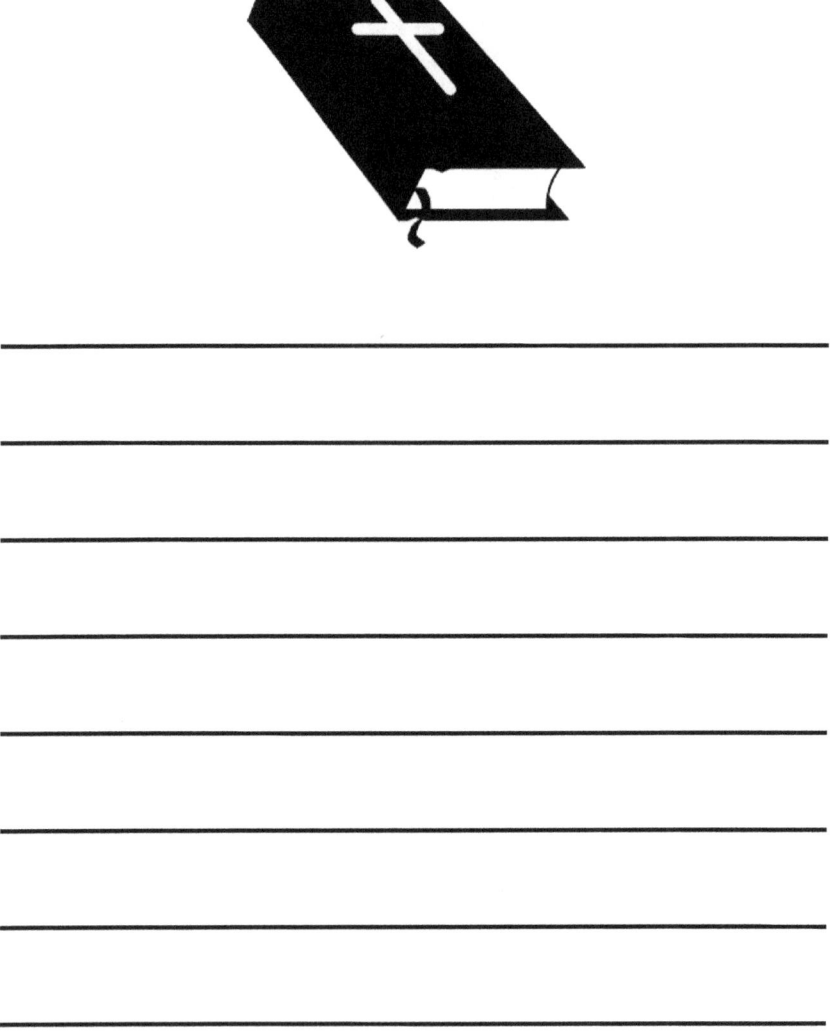

_____

_____

_____

_____

_____

_____

_____

GLEN R. LANDIN – GAIL A. REFFERT

GOD Is Infinite Blessings!

_____

_____

_____

_____

_____

_____

_____

GLEN R. LANDIN – GAIL A. REFFERT

GOD Is Infinite Blessings!

GLEN R. LANDIN – GAIL A. REFFERT

GOD IS INFINITE BLESSINGS!

GLEN R. LANDIN – GAIL A. REFFERT

GOD Is Infinite Blessings!

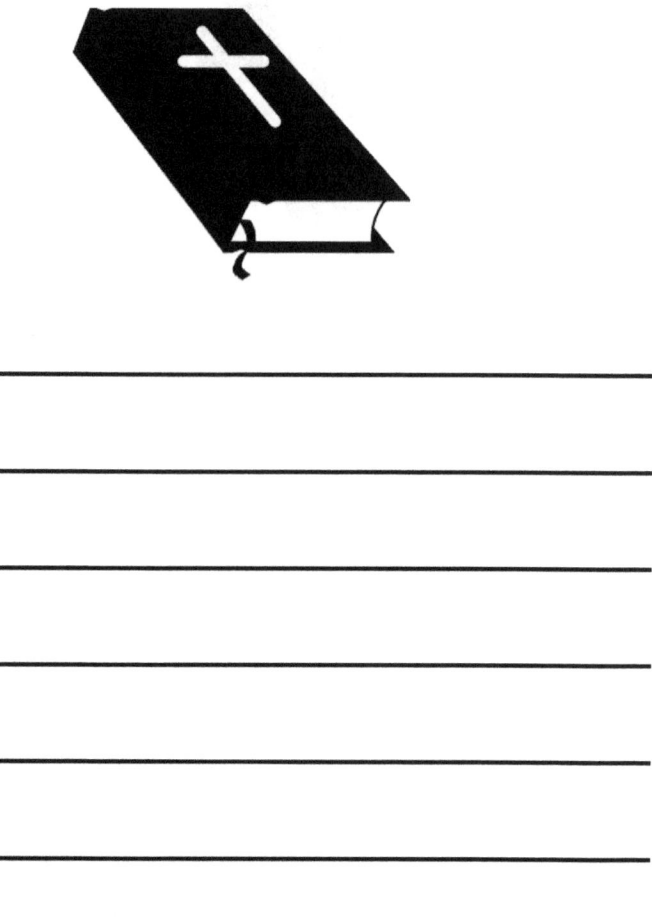

GLEN R. LANDIN − GAIL A. REFFERT

GOD Is Infinite Blessings!

GLEN R. LANDIN - GAIL A. REFFERT

GOD IS INFINITE BLESSINGS!

ABOUT THE AUTHORS

GLEN R. LANDIN HAS AN AA IN INTERIOR DESIGN AND LIVES IN CALIFORNIA. HE CONTINUES WRITING UNIQUE AND INFORMATIVE BOOKS. HE ALSO CREATES CANVAS AND PANORAMIC PRINTS. HE IS AN AUTHOR, PHOTOGRAPHER, DESIGNER AND CREATIVE ARTIST. THROUGH GLEN'S CREATIVE WRITING SKILLS, USING POEMS, PHRASES, AFFIRMATIONS, AND MESSAGES, HE INSPIRES, AND MOTIVATES OTHER PEOPLE TO BELIEVE.

THE GRACE OF OUR LORD JESUS CHRIST BE WITH YOU ALL. AMEN. – REVELATION 22:21

GAIL A. REFFERT GRADUATED FROM CAL STATE LONG BEACH WITH A BA IN LIBERAL ARTS AND A MINOR IN RELIGIOUS STUDIES. SHE MOVED TO ARIZONA AFTER BRAIN SURGERY IN 2001, AND SHE IS STILL SEIZURE FREE. SHE ALSO WROTE TWO PREVIOUS BOOKS, "COPING WITH BRAIN SURGERY" 2005 AND "INSPIRATIONAL THOUGHTS" 2007. SHE IS AN AUTHOR, SPEAKER, SINGER- SONGWRITER, AND PHOTOGRAPHER. GOD IS EVERYTHING TO HER.

BE STILL AND KNOW I AM GOD – PSALMS 46:10